Shafts of Sunlight in Redwood National Park

Crescent City Beach and Lighthouse

Tallest Tree in the World, 367.8', (112.1m.)

Foxglove

Humboldt Redwoods State Park

Fog on the Eel River Valley

Carson Mansion, Eureka

Mendocino Coast

Founder's Grove

Trinidad Lighthouse

Simpson Reed Grove, Jedediah Smith Redwoods State Park

Redwood Rhododendrons

Winter Redwoods

Skunk Train, Willits – Fort Bragg

Hidden Beach, Redwood National Park

Autumn in the Redwoods

Giant Burl

Redwood Sorrel (Oxalis oregona)

Redwood Brook

Richardson Grove

Mouth of the Klamath River

Roosevelt Elk

Fern Canyon

Unusual Root System

Diogenes Lanterns

The Fisherman, Eureka

Redwood Burl, Jedediah Smith Redwoods State Park

Trinidad Beach

Gingerbread Mansion, Ferndale

Henry Cowell Redwoods State Park